One Man's Utopia

by

S. Hayden Lovelace

PublishAmerica
Baltimore

© 2008 by S. Hayden Lovelace.
All rights reserved. No part of this book may be reproduced, stored in a retrieval system or transmitted in any form or by any means without the prior written permission of the publishers, except by a reviewer who may quote brief passages in a review to be printed in a newspaper, magazine or journal.

First printing

PublishAmerica has allowed this work to remain exactly as the author intended, verbatim, without editorial input.

ISBN: 1-60474-193-7
PUBLISHED BY PUBLISHAMERICA, LLLP
www.publishamerica.com
Baltimore

Printed in the United States of America

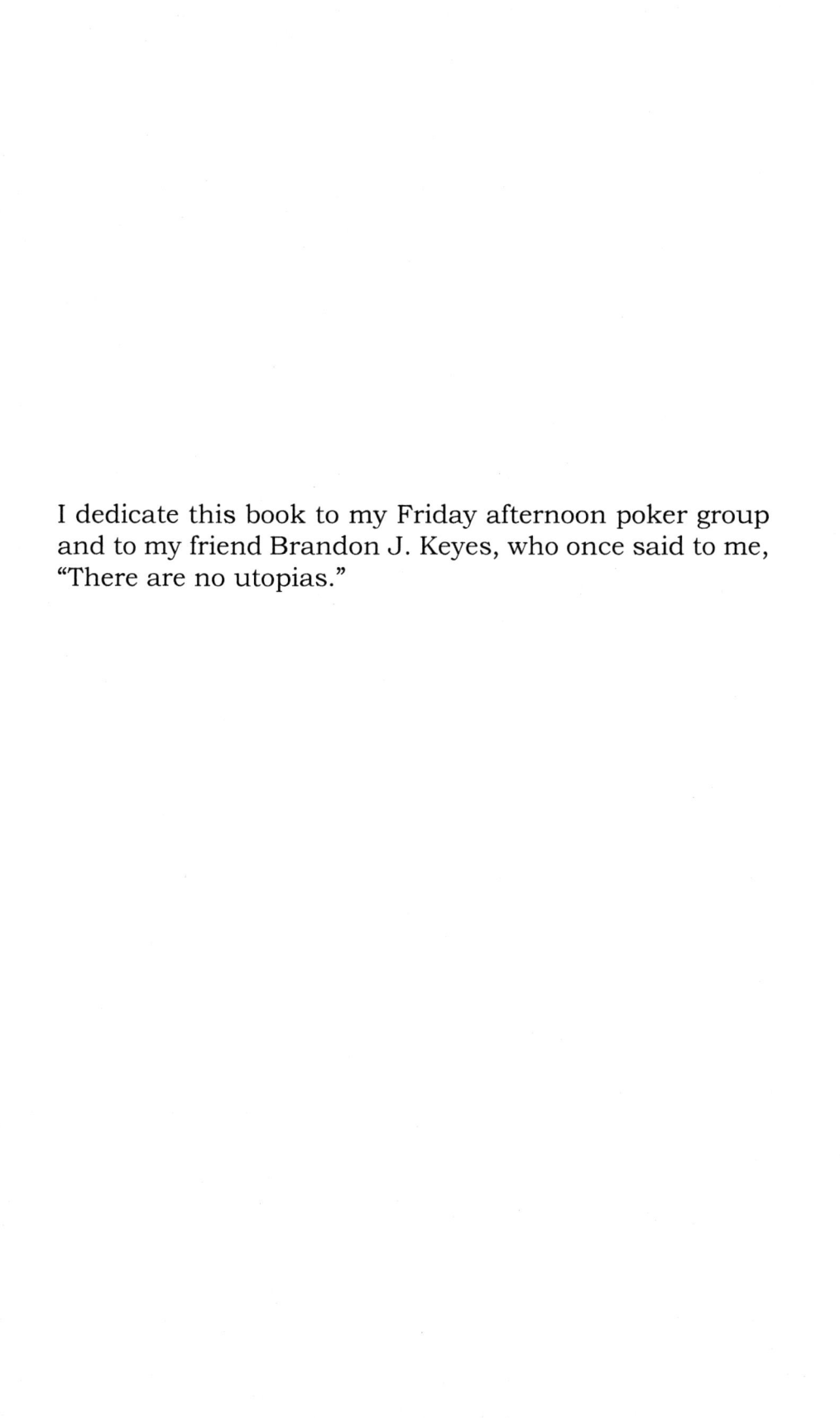

I dedicate this book to my Friday afternoon poker group and to my friend Brandon J. Keyes, who once said to me, "There are no utopias."

Introduction

This book is my opinion, my viewpoint, and contains a lot of attitude; it is from one angry American taxpayer to another angry American taxpayer. These pages are intended to be a quick and easy read. No filler words, no empty paragraphs, and no wasted paper! No soft peddling, no nonsense. I am shooting straight from the hip. That's all we have time for. I think it's time for us, the American voter and taxpayer, to take back our country. Make all elected and appointed politicians explain why we, the American people, are over nine trillion dollars in debt to China, Japan, Russia, and others! Why is all our stuff broken; our military, our Social Security, our Medicare, our educational system, our environmental climate, our national debt, our immigration laws, our drug laws, and our medical for the poor? It's time to stand up and say no more. We want our country back! I know the constitution has many good things, but it was written long ago when the illiteracy rate was high. We are smarter now and can see how evil, corruption, and greed are destroying our government and robbing us taxpayer's blind. It's time for a big change, and this is my utopia.

From this page on when I refer to the "Usual Suspects,"

I am talking about "Big Business," "Big Oil," and "Big Pharmaceutical;" all big monopolies and conglomerates. This book is about how to take back the United States of America from these privateers who are robbing the taxpayers blind while killing us with polluted water, toxic air, and a bankruptcy of our government. The usual suspects all fight every move to help slow down the global warming.

Foreword

In my opinion, we the American tax payers need to get down to the real problems facing this country. Rebuilding and modernizing our military from A to Z. Beefing up our National Guard and Coast Guard. China is modernizing a million-man army, is it true? After watching what's happening to us in Iraq, who knows? In my opinion, we have no self-defense army at home in the United States of America. Looking us in the eye are: worries of recession, self defense, global warming, health care, clean fuel, food production, coming water shortage, illegal immigrants, and a broken educational system. The way we sit right now if we were attacked I see a real mess—no army troops, no bullets, no equipment, no food, no border, no money, and no respect! Think this over, folks. We are unable to defend ourselves.

Let's get back to free enterprise, little factories for food processing and bullet making. Who ever heard of an army rationing out five or six rounds of bullets like they did in Iraq?

Let's start growing our own food again. We are importing way too much food. We need to be a lot more self reliant in our own country. We can once again be the strongest, smartest, richest, and most respected country in the world, if we make some tough decisions and take off our rose colored glasses. We also should grow and manufacture our own medicine by starting little pharmaceutical labs. Remember free enterprise? It's going to be hard for farmers to get money to plant clean fuel crops and build refineries because most banks are owned by the usual suspects.

We should stand up by the millions and demand our government do something now to slow global warming. By the way, the usual suspects are already trying to buy all the water rights they can. In my opinion, in time we will pay five dollars a gallon for water, just like we are paying almost four dollars a gallon for gas today. Also, the usual suspects are the one percent of the world's richest people.

Dreams for a Greater America

Take back our country from debt, illegal immigrants, drug dealers, privatizing our military, and of course the usual suspects. We the Americans, have a land mass for growing clean fuel crops that is bigger than many countries, from the Rocky Mountains to the Great Lakes and from the Canadian border to the Gulf of Mexico. Instead of giving farmers subsidies not to plant, we could, in all reality, become the first producers and exporters of clean fuel to the world. If we could get our government to back our farmers with money to plant clean fuel crops and build refineries, we could, in two years, "not ten or fifteen," start to slow global warming. We have enough capped fossil fuel in this country to mix the formula. The real reason we can't get money to do this with is because one of the usual suspects, "Big Oil," is putting their foot on the necks of the politicians they helped elect with big money contributions. They want their money back by voting against clean fuel crops and refineries for farmers. We also need converters for all cars, trucks, planes, tanks, ships, etc. Why not put up a reward for inventors for the best converters for vehicles being driven today? I'll tell you why, in my opinion, the usual suspects would see the handwriting on the wall. All the usual suspects' profits would be gone from war, privatizing, and medicine. Why do you think military hospitals are rat holes? Because they are all being privatized to one of the usual suspects, "Big Business." Why do you think the war on drugs cost billions of dollars a year, paid for by the taxpayers? In my opinion, it's because the usual suspect, "Big Pharmaceutical," says no to legalizing. They want to buy all their poppies from Iran, Pakistan, Afghanistan, and Turkey, where they can get them cheap and sell them back to us at horrific costs. And war? Who keeps an army at war moving? Another usual suspect, "Big Oil." How much fuel do you think it takes in gas and oil for generators, field hospitals, planes, trucks, tanks, jeeps, etc to run a war today? How much medicine today, just for the sick and the wounded? And lastly, usual suspects' food, vehicles, planes, tanks, tents, clothes, guns, gear, etc? Who takes care of all this; plus commissary workers, cooks, janitors? "Big Business." This suspect also supplies private small armies to protect civilian workers. The news reports an estimated eight hundred or more private companies in Iraq. All paid for by whom?

I want a politician to run, that can answer my questions. I want to know how we are going to pay off nine trillion dollars in national debt! How many trillions do we owe China, Russia, Japan, England, and others? What happens if China calls in the debt? Do we change our name to "Dumbellstan," Providence of China? I want to know how much Midwest farmland is being bought up by Arabs with American sounding business names. I want to know how long pharmaceutical companies are going to buy poppies from Afghanistan, Pakistan, Iran, and Turkey. When is the usual suspect, "Big Pharmaceutical" going to stop supporting war lords, the Taliban, al-Qaeda, Hamas, and others by buying up all these poppy fields from war lords? Why can't our farmers grow poppies to make medicine for our pharmaceutical companies?

When are we going to have term limits? When do we outlaw lobbyists? What's wrong with bringing back free enterprise for the little guy? How about small factories making dog food, toys, "clocks that work," etc? How about Mexico aid money for the twelve to fifteen million illegal immigrants going back home? How do we give foreign aid to other countries when we are going bankrupt ourselves?

When is health care for all Americans going to be a fact? When is education through college for every American child going to be a fact? Why aren't we already working to slow global warming?

While our corrupt government wallows in puffed up importance, the usual suspects are turning us into a third world country. The usual suspects now run our country and our elected politicians are their puppets. It's time for a champion for a term; someone who can cut through all the corruption and come straight to the people for decisions on important issues to be voted on by the masses, not just by the House and Senate. Every vote counts, yes or no; no more electoral votes! Let us hear freedom ring from corruption in government and the usual suspects.

A couple of last questions... Who is getting the money from Iraq's oil pipeline? What happened to the money? Wasn't that money supposed to pay for the war in Iraq? Is it true that millions, maybe even billions of dollars are missing from pipe line sales? Who is handling the bookkeeping and cash, America or Iraq? Why can't politicians talk about this?

Let's find a new strong leader, not business as usual politicians. What I wouldn't give to find one honest, intelligent, patriotic American to run under champion for a term. We the American voter, need answers too! How do you fix what is broken? And, where is the money coming from?

Well, I see I'm getting long winded here, so it's time to move on to more of my gripes.

Economy

I hate being treated like I can't count!
The National Debt...

Folks, we are nine trillion dollars in debt. By the time this book gets published, it will be ten trillion or close to it, maybe even more. We need a drastic change immediately in how our tax dollars are spent. How humiliating, we owe nine trillion dollars to China, Russia, Japan, England, and others. We need to be the richest country in the world. We are now heading for bankruptcy at full speed. If China calls in our debt, the good old USA could have a new name, "Dumbellstan, Providence of China." Politicians should not be handling our budget. We need economists to control and budget our tax dollars. Not one more dime to "Big Business," "Big Oil," and "Big Pharmaceutical."

Let's start putting real high duty on all imports from companies who moved their factories overseas. Why should we tax payers of America pay hundreds of dollars for something made in a third world country for hundreds of cents? Why not start up new small companies that pay above minimum wage, and a healthy amount of Social

Security for retirement along with subsidized medicine and subsidized education for children through college; people below the poverty line could flourish and private enterprise could once more put some backbone into our country.

When we are told the USA has only a five percent unemployment rate, that's a lot of horse puckey. What they don't tell you is that they count people that work part time or are working two or three jobs just to stay alive, and people that are only working a few hours a week. They also only count people that are actually looking for work as unemployed. Our government should count how many people are working full time, how many are working for minimum wage and below, and how many just aren't working. This is how I think we could turn the eminent bankrupt USA into a cash cow USA... Put economists in charge of our national debt and in charge of our national budget. Reduce retirement checks to retired politicians down to the national average. "No pork" on any bill passed through the House and Senate. No subsidies to "Big Business," "Big Oil," or "Big Pharmaceutical." Give subsidies to small businesses for start-up seed money. Give subsidies to farmers that produce clean fuel crops, poppy fields, food, etc. Give subsidies to new refineries for clean fuel. Give subsidies to inventors of converters for vehicles now driven, flown, or floated. Legalize drugs. Tax and build rehabilitation centers. Put all able bodied prisoners to work. They can pay for their upkeep, and do all the work illegal immigrants now do. They also can pay their child support and restitution to victims, along with paying taxes and Social Security. Export clean fuel. Be the first to slow global warming. Earn back respect and admiration of the world. We are hated now. We the people must stand up and shout for change! Real change, not the same old politician doing business as usual. We need a new leader, someone who will stand up for the people and not to the usual suspects and their puppets.

Here it comes... How much would it cost to have subsidized medicine? Subsidized education? And a have a well equipped military? I can only guess but I would say about forty to fifty cents on every dollar. But think this over. What would you pay for military protection and medical and education for your whole family? What are they worth to you?

I could be wrong about the cost, because if we stop the hemorrhaging of tax dollars to fighting three lost wars, it might not cost that much at all. That money could go to building up our military and subsidizing medicine and education. And with cutting away corruption, pork, and huge subsidies to the usual suspects, who knows we could have it all and lower taxes.

You investors out there need to move all your stocks out of crude oil and reinvest in the future of clean fuel, water, green crops of food, refineries, and small new pharmaceutical labs and plants. We need to become the Arabs of the West with clean fuel and water.

New energy of all kinds needs to be invented here in America. Remember folks, mass production drives prices down, not up. We will have the cheapest clean fuel in the world.

How to Finance Change and Keep the Economy from Imploding

Stop all subsidies to conglomerates. This along would save billions in tax dollars. Let the conglomerates pay their employees with the millions in sector profit they now pocket! Why should the tax payers pay the wages with tax money subsidies? Instead of giving millions to already rich oil companies for oil exploration, why not give millions to building new clean fuel refineries and towards the planting of clean fuel crops here at home? "Now!" Not fifteen years from now.

We, the tax payers, are not supposed to be smart enough to know that mass production drives prices down, not up. The more clean fuel we produce, the more we will have for exporting and the cheaper the fuel will become! This also will put us in the front of the line to slow global warming.

What about the millions of us that can't use clean fuel? That's what inventors are for. Put up a ten million dollar prize for the best convertors invented to run clean fuel in cars, trucks, planes, trains, and ships that we use today.

We, the American citizens, can do anything we put our minds to. Remember American know how? Well, another word for that is common sense. There are cultures in this world that do not have "know how" and our government has no common sense at this time. We need to encourage economists to run for House and Senate, they are people who really know how to budget, instead of attorneys and businessmen who know all the loopholes, including how to hide assets like blind trust and not paying their share of taxes.

What happened to the money from the oil pipeline in Iraq? Wasn't that money meant to help pay for the war? What about profiteers and private armies us tax payers are paying for in Iraq and other places? By stopping the three wars, the Middle East, illegal immigration, and illegal drugs, we would have enough funds to start to rebuild the American economy, along with subsidizing medical, building up the military self-defense against terrorism, and improving our educational system. Bring some common sense back into our government!

We are hemorrhaging billions of tax dollars to special interest groups, bail outs, greed, and corruption. This money alone, would keep this economy from collapsing.

Let's face it, America needs a strong, intelligent,

honest, determined, patriotic champion with a love of humanity to run for President; a person who is able to get over the heads of House and Senate and go directly to the people for votes to reform our government.

If the President and the people want the House and Senate to work on subsidized medical, the House and Senate have to make subsidized medical their number one priority. Let the people tell the government what to work on.

The House and Senate both have to make a list of priorities...

First, our economy: Solve how to build new free enterprise with no more subsidies to the usual suspects. Pump subsidies into mass production of clean fuels to use here at home and to export around the world, stimulating new revenue for our treasury.

Second, our military: Let the military order what they need instead of politicians telling them what they need, causing billions of dollars of inventory to be piled up in warehouses that cost millions to maintain, all for profit in a company that that politician has stock in.

Third, universal medical: Make it happen! The lower class continues to struggle while the upper class relaxes with ease as their medical coverage is paid for by our tax money.

Fourth, immigration: Let citizens vote on this, exodus or stay!

The list continues on and on...

We, the people, are supposed to tell our elected officials what we want, not have the elected officials tell us what we get by voting for special interest whims, instead of what is important to us, the taxpaying citizens of America.

Military

What about the scamming of the military war in Iraq? I hope this war is over by the time this book is published, if not, shame on America. By now, I hope troops are in Afghanistan or at home. I hope we are rebuilding our military back to the strongest in the world. Let's put all the tax money for military on the front burner and keep it there. For the last thirty or forty years big cuts in funding have been the norm. Our government has cut spending for equipment, modernizing, troop pay, disability payments, medical, and V.A. hospitals.

Hey folks, these are the guys who make it possible for us to live in a nice house, sit in a Lay-Z-Boy, watch big screen football, sleep in a fluffy bed with clean sheets, and eat fresh food imported from all over the world. Now, the wonderful government wants to privatize the commissaries so under paid, low ranking troops can pay more for their groceries. Do you know that low ranking troops are using food stamps and WIC cards to feed their families? I think we should put a stop to humiliating the troops who fight and die for us every day. Let's let the military go back to taking care of itself; washing its own clothes, cooking its own food, and cleaning its own toilets.

Why should privatized usual suspects be paid at least five times more than what a G.I. makes? That's b.s. for G.I.s. Our tax dollars pay these profiteers billions to work, "taking care of our military." Why don't we let the military have the billions to take care of themselves, starting with higher wages, better medical facilities, and rehabilitation centers for both physical and mental recovery? Instead, the usual suspects pass them on down to the next usual suspect who puts them on strong drugs and sends them home; that way, the hurt G.I. can buy his drugs from a pharmacy for the rest of their life, giving a usual suspect, "Big Pharmaceutical," a lifelong customer. God forbid the G.I. grow pot in his back yard for his pain, it would be free!

Our equipment is old and broken, patched together as best as possible. Why? Because military funds have been cut to the bone for decades. Giving money that should go to the military to usual suspects for privatization, that's how our politicians pay back for the huge contributions. Washington tries to make a big show by having the pentagon's top military brass fire service men they put in charge of administration of rat hole hospitals. Instead, why don't these high brass officials stand up and shout for all Americans to hear— "We have no money! We have been refused funds by our government for years and years!" In my opinion, they can't say anything because it means they will be forced to retire, be fired, have their reputation destroyed, and/or lose a retirement that they have worked a lifetime for. I wish just one of you guys from the pentagon would step forward and get on every talk show on television and tell the truth about the hospital rat hole disaster. Why can't congressmen and senators come forward and say we are trying to privatize the military and V.A. hospitals to the usual suspect "Big Business?"

The war in Iraq took them by surprise and they didn't

have time to get their dirty deeds done before the American public found out what they were doing.

Paying off the usual suspects for huge campaign contributions, in my opinion, this is how it works... "Big Business" buys a military facility, say a hospital. The hospital is paid for by low interest loans from our federal government; your and my tax dollars. Now the hospital is privately owned; the hospital now can charge any amount they want to our government for the care of military servicemen. This is paid for by our tax dollars as well. Now suspect one brings in suspect two; hospitals must have fuel to stay afloat. All energy is paid to suspect two. Now what is a hospital without drugs? Enter suspect three. Of course all care and drugs are paid for by our government, again, the hospital has been neglected by the military for so long it can be sold to suspect one for almost nothing. But, our politicians will make sure in the house that suspect one is given plenty of federal aid to rejuvenate that old rat hole the military failed to keep up.

Why can't all that money go to the military to fix its own hospitals? Yes, I am one pissed off tax payer! No more scamming of the military!

We need to go after al-Qaeda, the Taliban, and all terrorists groups. Pakistan seems to have no interest in finding Bin Laden. Their only interest is taking millions of dollars from our now empty coffers, so we can call them our allies. Pakistan is protecting terrorists instead of confronting them.

The fact is we started a war with the wrong country for the wrong reasons. We should leave Iraq, move our troops to Afghanistan, hopefully to the border of Pakistan, and really go after terrorists. If Pakistan refuses us, we should warn them that we will be sending rockets at their Afghan border.

We need our troops to come home!

Immigration

I do not hate illegal immigrants; rather, I want them to get into our country legally. Stop all the illegal immigrants today! Start by fining business owners who employ illegal immigrants and/or confiscating their private and business property, then arrest and jail those business owners who continue to employ illegal immigrants.

Anyone who has even one illegal immigrant working for them should abide by certain rules. First offense should be a loss of business license. I know this sounds harsh and cruel, but if we are going to stop the flood of people coming across our border in the southwest, we must make America a "do not want to go there" country! Make it as unpleasant as we can; no work, no hospitals, no school, no welfare, no apartments, and no housing. If we can harden ourselves to do this, "tough choice" people will stop coming here. Why are we building fences? They are digging tunnels. We must get tough and put a stop to illegal aliens flooding across our border. We can win this war and never fire a shot. How will we fill all these jobs done by illegal immigrants? We have jails, work farms, and prisons full of able bodied men and women.

Remember why we have to do this, "to make all Americans strong, safe, healthy, and financially on the rebound." To help Mexico with the exodus of twelve to fifteen million people coming back to their own country, foreign aid is appropriate for our neighboring Mexico to set up camps with food, shelter, and gas for all to get home.

In the states, the Red Cross, Salvation Army, churches, and all other humanitarians volunteer to hand out food, milk, medicine, water, toilet paper, gas, etc for the trip home. This would be paid for by our government, the "tax payers' money." It will take millions to do this exodus. We can blame mismanagement of that money, never used to secure our borders.

(You know things that are important to us the people).

How do we get the fields hoed and weeded? How do we get vegetables and fruit picked? My opinion on that is in my gripe on prison reform.

Social Security

I hate the government robbing Social Security. It's a shame the way Social Security is ripped off, not only do politicians dip in along with the President, but the wealthy and upper middle class draw it until they die. Dipping must stop! Many lower class and poor people only have Social Security to retire on. In my opinion, anyone retiring on over sixty thousand dollars or more a year should have a one-time pay out; all money they have paid into Social Security. Any person or couple making over eighty thousand dollars a year must also give up Medicare, and pay for private health insurance. Wealthy people do not need to draw Social Security at all, and should be more than happy just to get their money paid "back in full."

Medicare must be policed, the rip-off from medical suppliers alone is astounding, things delivered I don't want or don't need, I'm told, "that's a part of the package and I have to deliver it. "Don't worry you are not paying, Medicare is!" This is going on all over the country. How much is this costing the tax payer per day? Seems to me they should have inspectors going to homes and asking recipients if deliveries are only what is needed.

And while I'm talking about Medicare, how about free medical for everyone? Taxes would go up, but we could also cut fat off the budget. What if we have subsidized medicine for everyone who makes less than sixty thousand dollars a year? It would work like this... The government, "we tax payers," would educate doctors at tax payers' expense for families who make less than sixty thousand dollars a year. In return for schooling, young doctors would work in subsidized medicine for the poor for five years or so. Then, he or she would be licensed to work in private medicine. The same could be done with nurses, x-ray technicians, etc. This is just something to think about.

In my opinion it makes sense.

The War on Drugs and Poppy Fields

I hate being treated like I have an IQ of fifty. First, I want the usual suspect, "Big Pharmaceutical," to stop brainwashing the American public with commercials about their children becoming substance abusers. Let's educate ourselves about addiction. Scientists now realize three out of every ten people have what is called an addictive personality. It's not caused by beer, wine, whiskey, pot, hash, tobacco, cocaine, heroin, opium, or even food. Addictive personality is caused by genetics. Scientists are now trying to find a way to get rid of this sick gene in people who have it. This gene can be passed on or inherited from family genes. It may take many years, so until then, we will need rehab centers. If ten people are in a room and all partake of any addictive drug three people will become drug abusers. They will try all drugs until they find the one they like best. That now becomes their drug of choice; these addicts will need rehab to educate them about the gene that makes them sick from drugs, including alcohol, our number one killer drug. Alcohol kills more people each year than all other drugs combined. Now, let's look at the other seven people in the room, they do not have the addictive gene. They can partake of any or all the drugs and not get addicted.

People like to relax and feel good. But, what about the millions of people who have diabetes? They can't partake in alcohol because of too much sugar. So they go to their doctor and ask for a prescription for whatever makes them stop the pain or just feel good. There are many "feel good" drugs. Your doctor is happy to write a prescription, because he or she probably owns stock in a pharmaceutical company. Now you take the prescription to your pharmacy. Many people also pick up at the pharmacy, their insulin, high blood pressure medications, heart medications, cancer medications, etc.

Why can't they buy pot at a pharmacy? Let each state grow and tax its own pot and poppies. Taxes should pay for rehab hospitals and centers. Keep it cheap, so street dealing won't pay. States can tax farmers for poppy fields sold to a pharmaceutical company. If the big companies don't want to pay American prices, fine, start up small companies to make medicine. What makes and keeps this country strong is competition and free enterprise. Farmers need cash crops, poppies, clean fuel, fresh food, and pot. "We want free enterprise back!"

These usual suspects pay warlords for poppy fields, in turn; the warlord takes the money and supports the Taliban, al-Qaeda, and other terrorist groups who kill our troops. You don't have to be a rocket scientist to figure out that "Big Pharmaceutical" is backing the Taliban, al-Qaeda, and other terrorists. Why hasn't "Big Pharmaceutical" asked our farmers to grow poppy fields? Because in my opinion, there's not enough profit margin.

Do you have any idea how many millions of dollars leave this country every day from the sale of illegal drugs? Millions of people are using these drugs. Why should we let drug money go to Mexico, Central America, and South

America? We are supporting drug lords instead of using the money for farmers and rehab centers.

Remember seven of ten people using these drugs are social users, now called recreational users, not "addicts." And think of the millions of dollars going to Afghanistan, Pakistan, Iran, and Turkey from our biggest in the world drug dealers, pharmaceutical companies.

I'm getting angry just sitting here and thinking about the profit and loss in the drug trade to us tax payers. Medicare is paid for by tax payers, so tax payers now pay for feel good drugs that you can grow in your back yard, it's just a plant. You don't have to smoke it, you can eat it. Wake up tax payers, you have to know the world is using drugs, and instead of hemorrhaging tax dollars to fight a drug war "lost twenty years ago," use your reasoning ability. The pharmaceutical companies do not want any competition; they have the world monopoly on drugs and do not want any free enterprise. Free enterprise would mean they would have to drop prices.

Free enterprise is what this country used to be built upon. But, now this usual suspect has cornered the world market on drugs. "We should legalize, grow, and tax drugs!"

Let's look at the other side of the coin; "no to legalization." Let's keep paying billions of our dollars to fight drugs. After all, we do catch eight percent of drug smugglers. Guard the borders! We can pay agents, rent helicopters, and pay pilots to spy over wooded areas, corn fields, and people's back yards to see if they have a pot patch. We can buy planes to fly along approximately fifteen hundred miles of border to check for drug smugglers, we can build a high fence to keep out drugs and illegal immigrants. But, what about the two, three, and more mile tunnels the illegal immigrants are digging? We don't need to pour more tax money into a high fence, that's for sure!

In my opinion, while the illegal aliens are digging their way into our country, we are digging our way to bankruptcy. The war on drugs and immigration is not working and the laws have been broken for decades. If I were king of the mountain, this is what I would do... Make contributing to the delinquency of a minor, under the age of eighteen, a Class A felony; ten days in jail, this includes parents, before bail can be posted. Then, a new law would require all families with minor children, or anywhere children are welcome, to confine all firearms, alcohol, tobacco, drugs, and pornography under lock and key. Put teeth in this law. Think of how nice it would be if little Joe or Susie could go to a friend's house after school and not get shot, drunk, stoned, or molested. (Molested comes under the gripe on judicial systems.)

It's time for every voting, taxpaying American to sit down and think, educate, and inform yourself with all the facts you can find. We the people have to make the changes. Our politicians are just dancing puppets for the usual suspects. They will not change a thing; they want to talk about what they are going to do, but how much change? And where is the money coming from? And how are they going to fill up our bankrupt coffers? They could care less about us as a nation; they feel safe talking about morality issues like gay rights, abortion, and things the states will end up voting on. They don't want to talk about how to turn the drug problem around into a money maker, instead of a money breaker.

Who might be on my side in this? IRS, farmers, distributors, pharmacies, state tax revenuers, people that have been waiting for room at a rehabilitation center for six months or longer, and millions of social users. I do not believe methamphetamines should be legal.

No kidding folks. Think about what you just read.

Think about the truth of the matter. When you go to a new doctor and fill out the questionnaire, what is one of the first few questions? I'll answer that for you. Do you use recreational drugs? Most drugs users answer no, most alcoholics or people who drink responsibly say no, and even people who smoke tobacco say no. People are afraid to admit that they use recreational drugs in fear of jurisdiction against them. This skews the data provided from those questionnaires.

The guesstimate of Americans over the age of fifty-five using recreational marijuana is forty million or more. Think of how much tax money that would raise, and that's just the over fifty-five crowd. These people are pleasure users, not addicts.

In some states, where medical marijuana is legal, doctors are afraid to write a prescription for pot because Federal agents can arrest them and destroy their lives. The usual suspects are behind this, it stinks of Hitlerism to me.

When are states going to demand respect for their laws? State laws first (the people); Federal laws second (Big Brother). States that want to grow clean fuel crops, poppies, and pot for free enterprise should make new laws that supersede Federal laws. Let the people of the State vote, that's our right as Americans!

How to Shortcut the Breaking up of Monopolies and/or Conglomerates

Each state must demand specific state laws that supersede federal laws regarding free enterprise, stem cell research, the growing of poppies, legalized marijuana, etc. If a state votes yes for these items, then that law cannot be crushed by federal law. All the states need to do is pass a law, voted on by the residents of that state, and that law supersedes federal law. This alone will start to break up monopolies from the root up, instead of trying to take down corruption of the government from the top.

We the people can make a difference; all we have to do is vote for change at the grass roots level, "our state."

We will pay our federal taxes for military, Social Security, Medicare, subsidized medical, etc. However, each state will choose what it grows, builds, and/or legalizes.

No more big brother interference!

Environment

Let's stop handing out contracts to the usual suspects. Let us start by cleaning up toxic waste In order to do this; we must first put the right people in power. How about putting an environmentalist in office instead of appointing "Big Oil" puppets to oversee our environmental concerns? How about the health problems relating to lungs we now see in adults, small children, and even babies? Most caused by toxic air and toxic waste leaking towards people's water wells, creeks and rivers. Here we sit, waiting for a probable poison water disaster not demanding the government to clean up all pollution.

How about these changes... Make change to clean fuel now! Start growing clean fuel crops. Build refineries while crops grow. Train people to work in toxic waste cleanup. Close down the largest polluters. Explain and educate the public about the importance of using mass transportation. Put tolls on all freeways and heavily traveled arterials, but, free to mass transportation. Make all mass transit faster than driving oneself. We all need to pull together to slow global warming. Most ferries should be walk on, only freight and cars with more than one person for drive on. Grow millions of new trees; every family should either plant a few trees or pay to have trees planted. Clean up our water inlets, lakes, rivers, and bays. Put more inspectors in the field to check up on possible polluters and give them some clout. We need to conserve and harness our water supply and we need to do it now! With global warming, comes drought. We need water to live, grow crops, etc.

Water conservation should begin today so we won't have to pay five dollars per gallon! Let's make our government give start up money to individuals wanting to help clean up toxic waste, acid rain, and polluted water, individuals who want to conserve and harness water.

Remember free enterprise? Our big brother gives out contracts for this kind of work to the usual suspects and you see where that has put us. We need to pump some new "want to make it right" back into our country.

With free enterprise for the little guy, maybe we can regain some kind of respect from around the world.

Energy and Water Conservation

When late fall comes around, snow starts falling at high altitudes; this is the beginning of next summer's snow pack. Each time it snows in the mountains, the snow packs get deeper. In the spring, with warmer weather, the snow packs start to melt. Little creeks start forming and turn into bigger creeks as they flow down to rivers that flow to sea level. Along the way, lakes and reservoirs hold back the clean fresh water. We drink, bathe, wash clothes, water the lawn, and wash our vehicles with the water that is held back. This is parts of the country with no natural summer rainfall. About eight western states grow all crops with irrigation water.

Now with climate change, we find less and less snow pack because the mountains are having shorter and warmer winters. We have a lot of snow and then warm weather and rain. This causes the snow to melt and the water to run out into the sea. Lakes and reservoirs are dropping while the oceans are rising.

Here is an idea, why doesn't the government give states and counties subsidies to build small hydroelectric dams higher in the mountains? Not only to conserve water, but to make electricity at the same time. Oh, wait, I forget, we can't use common sense anymore! What about drilling for water as hard as we drilled for oil? Give big subsidies to water exploration.

In my opinion, the reason we can't get anything like this done is because one of the usual suspects, "Big Power," says no to subsidies for free enterprise in electric and water exploration. Only conglomerates and monopolies get the really big bucks.

Natural rainfall must be considered as well. As the climate gets warmer, there will be less rainfall. Rain barrels are needed at every American home; it should be as common as a garden hose. I would like to buy two or three good, strong, fifty gallon barrels, attractive with a spout close to the bottom, different colors, made in America, with name of city and phone numbers of factory printed on the barrels. America will buy!

Climate change is here and it's not going away. Here we sit, waiting for impending devastating droughts here in America. Why hasn't our government started preparing for droughts? In my opinion, it's because the usual suspects are busy buying up all the water rights they can so in less than ten years from now they can sell us water for ten dollars a gallon. Go ahead and laugh, today I paid over three dollars a gallon for gas. Who would have thought that five years ago?

In some towns in Australia people are down to one gallon a day per person! Whole towns are being warned that evacuation is possible soon because of no water! Is Atlanta far behind these Australian towns?

Let's start drilling for underground sources of water to irrigate our food crops and our new energy, clean fuel. Global warming is worldwide and drought exists in many countries. Other countries won't be able to produce our food and other products because they are running out of water just like we are.

Invest in energy and water exploration and conservation!

Term Limits

Stop the tide of greed and corruption! Let's get rid of professional politicians who are the puppets of the usual suspects. Professional politicians are people who look at service to their country as a way to get rich with high wages and whatever else they can get from the usual suspects such as contributions for their election or re-election campaign. These contributions include payoffs, graft, and all kinds of rewards for squelching any bill put to a vote that might give the American Joe or Jill a chance at free enterprise or trying new and inventive ways of getting away from fossil fuel, getting cheap medicine, and real environmental cleanup. By helping out the usual suspects with their vote, they also are guaranteed more money for their next run for office.

Also, let's not forget the hefty retirement and medical plans they receive. This has to stop! One term, with average pay, average retirement, and average Social Security. Only people who really care about America as a whole need apply. This is only my opinion. I would like to see the people all vote on this issue: term limits, yes or no?

Education

We need subsidized school for every legal American child, from preschool though college. And let's start having teachers that can think of interesting and stimulating ways to teach young children how to make choices. When a teacher walks into a first grade classroom, after saying, "Good morning children," their first question should be, "What would you like to do first this morning, reading or math?" And the children will take a vote and see what the majority wants. This should continue through intermediate school.

We need a group of educators to travel the world and find out who has the best teaching methods, the highest rate of graduates, and what country has the smartest pupils in the world. We should adopt systems that will excite, encourage, and stimulate our children to want to think and learn.

Is it true we are tenth to fifteenth in the world now for educating our children? And is our number in health care for the uninsured population somewhere close to or tied with Bangladesh at fifteenth? We need a better education system!

Prison Reform

Here is where we can save millions. Why should tax payers pay for prisons? Prisons should be self supporting. Why aren't prisoners out working the jobs illegal immigrants are doing? Why aren't they paying for their own keep, paying child support, paying victims' restitution, and paying Social Security? Employers of illegal workers should be able to go to city, county, or any other jail or prison and ask for workers and prisons should provide guards, to be paid out of prisoners pockets. Farmers should have work camps set up during planting and harvesting times, paid for out of prisoner's wages.

Why should tax payers pay to keep these guys lying in cells, lifting weights, watching television, and eating, many getting too fat to work? Prisoners can do fieldwork, orchard work, restaurant work, hotel work, cooking, cleaning, manual labor, and anything an illegal can do. And we taxpayers could save millions of dollars.

I would also separate the mentally ill from the common criminal. Take three prisons; put the mentally ill in one and make that a "hospital prison," the next prison would be for hard core prisoners that could not be let out to work, called "hard time prison," and the third would be a "work prison." This could be done on every scale from small jail to large prisons.

Also, the mentally ill, if given proper medications, could work and the hospital prison could be used in part as a half way house. I do not think that child molesters should be in prison, they should be executed or castrated and sent to a far off prison island where escape is impossible. They could have implements to build, seeds to plant, and care for small animals for food. We are told this is cruel and unusual punishment, b.s.!

What about the prisoners that refuse to work? Well let's see... Ah, yes, there are the good old chain gangs. Maybe we could use them for loafers. We have paid for the prison system for too long and we think that's okay, not me! I don't want my tax dollars paying for prisons anymore.

Again, what about free enterprise? Let people who think they can make a jail or prison profitable and self supporting get start up money low interest loans from our tax dollars. Anyone doing this would be accountable to the government for all prisoners, work hours, paid wages, health, dental, etc and free access to any prisoner at anytime. This all can be done quickly. The hard core prisoners can be put on chain gangs with guards and worked growing food and taking care of animals, milking cows, etc. That's how they can help support the prison.

Big brother says we can't make these changes over night, why? Because you have to go through all the red tape, delays, and road blocks that will be put up by the usual suspects, the big boys who supply prisons with food, bedding, uniform, medicine, fuel, etc. God forbid a prison become self-sufficient. How many millions would we save in tax dollars?

Well, these are just ideas that cross my mind. After all, it is just my view of things.

P.S. Just the offenders paying child support would take a huge load off the welfare system, resulting in more tax money to pay for medical and education.

Foreign Aid

No more cash to foreign governments. Why can't we, as a nation, give foreign aid that consists of food, medical, building supplies for schools and hospitals, seeds, tractors, fertilizer, well digging and irrigation equipment, and good old American know how? Instead of giving money, let America build all equipment needed for foreign aid, then the government could use our tax dollars to buy the equipment and send it as foreign aid. All foreign aid should be distributed by Americans, by either humanitarians or military workers. All equipment, food, medicine, etc should be painted red white and blue with USA stamped on every item. It's time to start beating Hamas and other terrorists at their own game.

Mexico will be very much in need of foreign aid when millions of people flood back across the border. This aid includes food, medicine, sleep and shower facilities, fuel, bus transportation for people on foot, ambulances for the sick or injured, and building supplies. It's time for Mexico to build its economy instead of sending all their hungry people to America.

Mexico needs to turn its deserts into irrigated farm land by drilling for water and harnessing its snow and rain fall. Yes, there are mountains in Mexico.

Why can't Mexico give its desert to the poorer people to start small farms? I think Mexico should be our number one priority for foreign aid, with no cash to government. Money for aid should be in the form of medicine, grown and/or manufactured in the USA by small start up pharmaceutical companies. That way the government would buy the medicine from new free enterprise startup companies instead of the usual suspects. The new pharmaceutical companies could buy the poppies from the farmer down the road instead of the warlords in Afghanistan who give their money to the Taliban to kill our troops.

Think about this just for a little, before you think I'm crazy... For disasters, earthquakes, floods, etc it would be the same program; no cash, rather send food, water, medicine, building supplies, and equipment to rebuild schools, hospitals, homes, water systems, electric plants, etc and everything built, grown, produced, and/or manufactured be from America, painted red, white, and blue.

I guess I could go on and on, but I did say I would keep this short. Think about how you would change our foreign policy. I can't say this enough, folks; we need free enterprise back big time! Foreign aid is one way to earn respect back from the world and beat Hamas at its own game at the same time.

Freedom of Religion

Our forefathers wanted us to have the freedom to believe in any religion we choose, that's why people of all religions live in America. All are welcome; Christianity, Judaism, Buddhism, Hinduism, Islam, etc. And under all major religions are many denominations. Under the Christian umbrella are all denominations that believe in Jesus Christ. Under the Buddhist umbrella are all who believe in Buddha. Under the Islamic umbrella are all who believe in Mohammed. And so forth down the list. And each denomination under all religions umbrellas believes just a little to a whole lot differently. But remember one thing, they all believe in a hereafter, they all call it a word in their own language; Christians call it heaven, Islam calls it paradise, Buddhists call it nirvana, etc.

Some Americans think Islamic terrorists are ignorant, backward, and desert rats. In fact, many are. Their education uses mostly radical to extreme religion. This is the bottom of the barrel for most Muslims. Muslims around the world are ashamed of these fanatics.

We also have the bottom of the barrel in Christianity right here in America. They twist the bible to fit their hate and extreme fanaticism. Their umbrella is called the Ku Klux Klan. They have names of their own; "Aryan Nation," "Posse Comitatus," "The Order," "The National Alliance," "11th Hour Remnant Messenger," "Aryan Brotherhood," and many others. This is why it's important to realize that in all the different religions and denominations there are people who are zealots and extremist, many working as teachers in private and public schools.

The religious zealots in America want a country run on religion. Why don't they go to Iran, Saudi Arabia, or Iraq to see how religion works with politics? We don't need a Holy War here in America. We need to keep our government for all the people and our religion in our heart and mind. Let's teach our children faith at home and at church, and let the schools teach reading, writing, math, social studies, etc. And let's teach our children to love other children no matter what color, culture, or religion they are. I do believe in separation of church and state.

We need our troops here at home to watch our own home grown terrorists, starting with the Ku Klux Klan and all its underlings teaching hate to their children.

It's time to clean our own corruption out of our government; a strong leader who is honest and patriotic would suit me.

This is my opinion.

Foreign Policy

In my opinion, the first thing an ambassador needs to know is diplomacy, knowledge of languages, cultures, and tradition. Next, and most important, is the mentality of the culture as a whole. We must always take this under consideration before talking to leaders around the world. For all we know, many dictators could have schizophrenia, or some other illness, and therefore cannot be trusted to sign peace or nuclear arms agreements or keep their word if they do sign. I think we should put our cards on the table and be honest and open in talks on world peace, global warming, world trade, and the war on terrorism. And only discuss these subjects with intelligent, open minded leaders.

The countries growing and/or supporting terrorist should be left out of the talks until changes are made. I have ideas about how to fight terrorism and I can only hope our government is smart enough to do half the things I've thought of; ideas not to be blabbed out in a book.

When appointing ambassadors, send a Chinese-American to China, a Mexican-American to Mexico, a Russian-American to Russia, etc. Forget party lines;

democratic, republican, etc. Let's put the most qualified person in the ambassador's chair. No more b.s. along party lines!

Domestic Issues

In my opinion, stem cell research is a way to help stop disease and stop millions of needless deaths. But this is also something that should be left up to each state to vote on. Each state: yes or no? Remember free enterprise?

Whistleblowers against all fraud should be rewarded. Witnesses against crime should be rewarded. People who help an injured person should be rewarded.

Each state could save millions by executing vicious violent offenders, murderers, rapists, and child molesters "in the courtyard, after sentencing." Family, friends, or a volunteer would perform the execution with two bullets to the head, at the cost of two dollars or less instead of two million or much more for each execution. In order to do this, it's up to the tax payers to vote on changing the judicial system in each state. We the people have to vote for new and stronger laws and sentencing. Judges must be able to put an offender away for life or give the jury the power to ask for immediate execution.

Our prison system is over-loaded with child molesters. They build new prisons with our tax dollars for drug dealers and drug users. Stop and think about this. We the tax payers can change this by putting the child molesters in the new jails and putting the drug people to work in place of the Mexicans going home to their own country.

Next, jury duty is something we all need to do if called upon. This is where your vote counts for sure. No one should get out of being called for a jury pool. And you young people, who are not registered to vote, will not be called for jury duty. You are giving up one of our most important rights.

Moving on, let's talk about the mentally ill. Many people living in the streets are mentally ill. In most cases they are so ill that they think everyone is crazy except themselves. Schizophrenia is a good example of people who think they are fine; it's the government, the FBI, the doctors, the aliens, etc who are crazy and trying to steal their brain by asking them to take poison. The poison being medication to help them stop the voices telling them all this b.s. Laws should be made to force the mentally ill to stay on their medication. Mentally ill should go to hospitals, not jail, for evaluation, anymore we just throw them into the street or into prison. What a shame for America to turn its back on the mentally ill. In my opinion, "we," the taxpaying, law abiding citizens, should demand rehabilitation centers for addicts and the mentally ill be put on a fast track now!

This also should be paid for with universal health care and/or subsidized medicine.

Now we should talk about abortion. In my opinion, it's time for men to get their nose out of women's vaginas and other reproductive organs. Women don't try to tell men what they can or can't do with their penis and testicles when it comes to accidental impregnation. Think about how silly this sounds.

Let's leave this issue to a man and a woman thinking of marriage to discuss. The unmarried woman should be able to make her own decision about her own body. If abortion has to come to a vote, then let each state vote.

Think about this people, how foolish is it to put important issues aside to debate abortion and same sex marriage, playing on religious emotions to keep your mind off things like war, global warming, medical care, Social Security, education, immigration, national debt, corruption in our leaders, and corruption in our government, House, and Senate?

Next, let's put a stop to domestic violence, child neglect, and abuse, be it verbal, emotional, or physical. To accomplish this, rewards should be paid to whistleblowers. Let's build some real good housing facilities for troubled children coming out of dysfunctional homes. Also, schools for parents to attend to learn good parenting is a good idea.

Who knows, maybe a majority could be reunited after educating both children and parents on how to recognize abuse instantly. Teach young children to report neglect or abuse by dialing 911 immediately. This could all be paid for by refusing to pay for wars lost twenty years ago.

"And no more bail outs to the usual suspects!"

This is How I See America

It's hard for me to go out and vote for a president knowing he or she has been campaigning on big money given by the usual suspects or if the campaigner is wealthy and owns lots of stock in the usual suspects. I know no change is going to happen. I asked my twenty-two year old grandson, in his last year of college, and already a navy reservist, if he is registered to vote. He said no! His vote was worthless as long as we have the Electoral College. He said most of his friends are of the same thought. We should put an end to these things immediately, strictly voted on by the people only: yes or no! Term limits? Lobbyists? Electoral Vote?

This would be a great start at cutting corruption on the hill. Of course, if anyone tried to do this, the politicians would start accusing the person of trying to destroy the Constitution. I don't think the Constitution should be done away with, however, I do think it should be updated by the people, with an amendment to rid all corruption, graft, and greed from House and Senate. No more deals with the usual suspects. No more pay raises, fancy medical packages, or big retirement umbrellas all done in the dead of the night while us "dummies" are asleep, and the next morning hear about it on the news. We say, "Oh well, what can I do about it?" How about stopping their entire medical coverage until everyone has it? And I don't want Mexico to hate the USA for sending back fifteen million hungry people, that's why we really need to end the war in Iraq, and take that money to exodus fifteen million illegal aliens back to Mexico and Central America.

And I really would hate to see killers, molesters, and rapists put to death, so we the people could start an adoption program. Everyone who is against the death penalty can then adopt a killer, molester, or rapist. They can pay for the prisoners keep, out of their pocket, because I am sick of my tax dollars going to support the criminally insane. I am sick of our tax dollars going to the usual suspects.

I'm tired of billions of tax dollars going to fight wars we lost twenty or thirty years ago. I'm tired of tax money going to pay high flying retirement for politicians. I'm tired of young people trying to work two or three jobs and go to school at the same time. I'm sick of seeing young G.I.s in line at the commissary using food stamps and WIC cards.

And let's keep the pulpit out of the House and Senate and keep the government out of the church and out of our homes and out of everyone's bedroom. Let's have a lot more private enterprise for small businesses. Let's have a strong and well equipped and well paid military. Let's have medical for every American and college education for every American. And next time we invade another third world country, let's attack with food, medicine, building supplies, candy bars, bubble gum, soccer balls, and tennis shoes. Let's try winning the hearts of the people instead of hatred. Let's start building water reservoirs owned by counties or states, not to be sold to or controlled by the usual suspects. Let's make our government clean up toxic waste by putting people to work instead of by giving all clean-up contracts to the usual suspects, who in turn, are receiving more and more money without much getting done. Money should come to each state and each county for clean up, no more contracts to out of state or out of county bids. Make people accountable right where we live, again cutting graft and corruption.

Let's fight AIDS with drugs grown and manufactured by startup pharmaceutical companies owned by small private enterprise. Let's be the first nation to export clean fuel and converters for everything that runs, flies, or floats. Let the new refineries be owned by small, independent farmers and from surrounding communities, never to be sold to profiteers. Profit from the refineries should go back into the communities. Let all the people in the communities vote on how to use the funds. You know, we should have free enterprise and freedom for each American to vote on issues that concern every tax dollar; including Federal, State, County, and city, wherever tax dollars are spent. Make all communities accountable for every dollar.

Our Constitution is two-hundred and twenty years old. As I understand it, the reason for it was that learned men in politics running the government believed the average voting American man, "women couldn't vote," was too illiterate to form an intelligent choice. That's how and why we still have the Electoral College, after two hundred and twenty years. Do you, the voting public, think we are now literate enough to have our vote counted? Why don't we just abolish the electoral voting system? Who are the electoral voters? The usual suspects' puppets of course.

We really need to update the Constitution, keep all the freedom stuff, privacy stuff, and cut out all the tricky stuff for the rich and powerful. Look how corrupt our House and Senate are. The world is now run by the usual suspects and their puppets. They are the politicians owning large blocks of stock in the usual suspects' businesses.

Let's let our college students know their own vote could put an end to electoral voting. No more politicians with blind trust. That means they don't know how much of their money has been invested in the usual suspects—all their money in most cases is stock in big corporations, oil, and pharmaceuticals. But, you say millions of people will be out of work if we stop giving billions in subsidies to the usual suspects. "No!" These very people can now go to work for private enterprise in new startup, free enterprise business. Men and women can join a military service with good pay, new equipment, decent housing, and good clean medical facilities. Giving out startup, low interest loans to small private enterprise will stimulate the blood of America. Make us strong and wealthy again.

Let's put all able bodies to work, put able incarcerated men and women to work. No more taxes to pay for prisons. Free enterprise can build small work camps with low interest loans from tax dollars. Let's put our tax dollars where our mind and our health are, in education and medical for everyone, and in safety for a strong, well equipped, and well paid military with excellent health facilities and towards a resilient homeland security plan.

I know I am riding this military thing to death, but we have to understand without a strong military, we are doomed. Give the military back to the military, and give money that's going to the usual suspects to the military. Cut the head off the snake called "privatized."

In my Utopia, our American President would go to China, Russia, England, Japan, Iran, and elsewhere with an olive branch to talk about nuclear energy, nuclear waste, and nuclear war. I think this is a very high priority!

My Utopia

This is my Utopia. I would like to see a president for a term with power over the House of Representatives and the Senate, what I mean by that is our champion president could order both of these bodies of government to work on legislation for universal medicine, Social Security, and the exodus of fifteen million illegal aliens.

Stop the wars: Iraq, drugs, and immigration. Stop all subsidies, except for farmers growing clean fuel crops, for the building of refineries for clean fuel and food, for the startup for the planting of poppy fields for medical, and for the startup for small pharmaceutical labs and food factories. Give subsidies to rehab centers for the mentally ill, drug addicts, and children from abused homes. Give foreign aid to Mexico with no cash to the Mexican government. And most of all, fix our military and self defense. Pay troops higher wages. If all subsidies stopped that go out to the usual suspects and other pork, corruption, and bailouts we would have the best paid troops in the world.In my Utopia, police and firemen would be paid very high wages, farmers and fuel producers would make a good living. In my Utopia, orphanages would be clean and well staffed with caring, educated, loving workers and volunteers from big brother, big sister, and lots of volunteer grandparents for all unwanted, unloved children. This would be the norm instead of foster care.

In my Utopia, every American would have medical and dental coverage, every child would have the right to a college education, and every legal American would register to vote and every vote would count.

In my Utopia, the United States would again become the envy of the world, respected and rich, the leader of exporting clean fuel. Pay off all national debts. Fight wars with food, tools, seeds, building materials, know-how, soccer balls, bubble gum, and coca cola.

In my Utopia, we would start digging huge lakes and building dams to hold water runoff from rain and melting snow. Global warming is no joke to laugh at. Snow pack is less and less every year.

In my Utopia, the US would be the leading country in the world to slow global warming, the US would be the first to have an honest, clean, corruption free government run by the people, for the people, the way it's supposed to be, term limits would be a fact, and politicians would receive average pay, no pork, no payoffs by the usual suspects, no big medical plans, and no big retirement.

In my Utopia, the USA would again produce enough food for the population plus export food, the USA would make its own shoes, clothes, clocks, etc, and prisons would be self supporting.

In my Utopia, poverty would be on its way out the door and corruption in government would become extinct.

In my Utopia, tax payers would vote on a champion president for a term, "no electoral college votes." I want a president who looks into the heart and soul of humanity, an intelligent patriot who loves his country and his fellow Americans. A champion for justice for all. A person who, above all, is honest with the ability not to abuse power. A champion with the capacity to do and act physically, mentally, legally, morally, and financially competent. My champion will have a natural skill for problem solving and be a communicator on all levels, including foreign policy. My champion will have the "I can bring this country back to greatness" mentality.

Final Words

Let's hope this coming election in 2008 will bring back some kind of decency away from corruption. But, I must admit, I am not enthusiastic about the outcome. So far they all smell of big contributions from the usual suspects. We are deadheading for no change.

About the Author: S. Hayden Lovelace

All you need to know about this author is that I am a tax paying, law abiding, voting citizen of Washington State. My first introduction to politics was sitting on my grandfather's knee listening to President Roosevelt's fire side chats. Next, I listened to President Truman on a whistle-stop at the union train station in Tacoma. As I grew up, I drifted away from all government issues. Now the last few years I have been paying close attention to the news, political arguments, news papers, and political corruption expos . I am so pissed off at myself and all other tax payers and voters. I decided to write this book and express my anger. When I asked my college educated grandson if he was registered to vote and he said no, (because as long as we have the Electoral College his vote would never count anyway) I knew I had to finish this book I have been dabbling with for over two years.

This book is written strictly from my gut. It is full of attitude, opinion, viewpoints, and anger. In my dream of Utopia, we the United States of America would again become the strongest, smartest, wealthiest, and respected nation in the world. We are now one of the world's biggest jokes. Our government corruption rivals all the dirtiest in the world. People around the world hate us. We have to have a change in government to bring respect and decency back to the American people.

The Constitution is two hundred and twenty two years old; it needs to be modernized for the future, starting with an amendment to stop all corruption in all three branches of government.

Let's get back to a Constitution for the people; all the people, instead of just the rich and greedy.